ADVANCE PRAISE FOR
*Pitchblende*

"In *Pitchblende*, Elise Marcella Godfrey's experimentation with poetic form and multiple voices, archival and imagined, to address the fallout of uranium mining that often places profit over ecology, community, and sustainability, is radiant. The poems are alive and magnified with testimony of Indigenous Elders, women, and activists, who are steadfast in their defense of Earth's inhabitants and life-giving forces. *Pitchblende* is 'against forgetting.' In her honest rendering of voices that are often diminished or dismissed, Godfrey has earned the name of ally." —RITA BOUVIER, author of *nakamowin'sa*

"*Pitchblende* is a distilled act of witnessing, built from nearly forgotten testimonies, half-erased voices, compromised lands and bodies. It speaks powerfully to our shared vulnerabilities as well as the deeply unequal legacies of environmental racism, settler-colonial amnesia, and corporate doublespeak. Language itself is irradiated in these stark poems, so that words, like isotopes, 'break down over time.' Yet the voices remain for us in uncanny, ghostly memory, speaking to the future we are making." —WARREN CARIOU, editor of *mahikan ka onot: The Poetry of Duncan Mercredi*

"In *Pitchblende*, Elise Marcella Godfrey gives us a beautifully layered poetic investigation of environmental degradation in the Anthropocene, focusing specifically on uranium mining and its consequences in Saskatchewan Treaty territories. Godfrey has taken transcripts of public hearings and reworked them into a range of poetic forms; in particular, she uses erasure as a form of intervention that troubles the discourse of industry and profit, 'tipping [the text] toward a precipice, toward misprision.' She highlights the voices of Indigenous women

and Elders, their testimony a chorus that warns and laments. Ranging from subterranean deposits to the planet and out to the stars, the poems draw on different areas of knowledge—history, geography, geology, cosmology, mythology, and more—creating a shimmer of perspectives and a heady reading experience. The imaginative leaps and the gorgeous sound play in these poems suggest that poetry can contribute to the increasingly urgent project of re-imagining our place on Earth."
—HILARY CLARK, author of *The Dwelling of Weather*

ᎣᏏᏲ
OSKANA POETRY & POETICS

# Elise Marcella Godfrey
## *Pitchblende*

University of Regina Press

© 2021 Elise Marcella Godfrey

All rights reserved. No part of this work covered by the copyrights hereon may be reproduced or used in any form or by any means—graphic, electronic, or mechanical—without the prior written permission of the publisher. Any request for photocopying, recording, taping or placement in information storage and retrieval systems of any sort shall be directed in writing to Access Copyright.

Cover art: "Skeleton fish" by designer_an / AdobeStock

Cover and text design: Duncan Campbell, University of Regina Press

Editor: Randy Lundy
Proofreader: Donna Grant

The text and titling faces are Arno, designed by Robert Slimbach.

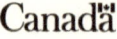

*Library and Archives Canada Cataloguing in Publication*

Title: Pitchblende / Elise Marcella Godfrey.

Names: Godfrey, Elise Marcella, author.

Series: Oskana poetry & poetics ; 12.

Description: Series statement: Oskana poetry & poetics ; 12

Identifiers: Canadiana (print) 20210230002 | Canadiana (ebook) 20210230029 | ISBN 9780889778405 (softcover) | ISBN 9780889778412 (PDF) | ISBN 9780889778429 (EPUB)

Subjects: LCGFT: Poetry.

Classification: LCC PS8613.O334 P58 2021 | DDC C811/.6—dc23

UNIVERSITY OF REGINA PRESS
University of Regina
Regina, Saskatchewan
Canada S4S 0A2
TELEPHONE: (306) 585-4758
FAX: (306) 585-4699
WEB: www.uofrpress.ca
EMAIL: uofrpress@uregina.ca

We acknowledge the support of the Canada Council for the Arts for our publishing program. We acknowledge the financial support of the Government of Canada. / Nous reconnaissons l'appui financier du gouvernement du Canada. This publication was made possible with support from Creative Saskatchewan's Book Publishing Production Grant Program.

*Pitchblende is dedicated to all land defenders and water protectors worldwide, and especially to Indigenous Peoples on the front lines.*

## CONTENTS

1   Follow the Water—*Délı̨nę, Northwest Territories*
2   The Rock Reveals Itself—*Délı̨nę, Northwest Territories*
3   LaBine—*Echo Bay, Great Bear Lake*
4   Pitchblende
6   Enter the Transcripts
7   Elder's Testimony—*Stony Rapids*
8   Inuit Tapirisat of Canada's Testimony *(Erasure)*
10   Lichenology
11   Caribou Conservation Board's Testimony *(Erasure)*
12   The North Is Not a Barren Land
13   Rabbit Lake Uranium Mine
14   When Women Speak—*Hidden Bay*
15   Ore Body
16   Elder's Testimony—*Black Lake*
17   Uraneco's Response—*Black Lake*
18   Dust or Pollen
19   Fond du Lac
20   Elder's Testimony—*Fond du Lac*
21   Uraneco's Response—*Fond du Lac*
22   Parse the Numbers
23   Hatchet Lake Band's Testimony *(Erasure, Part One)*
26   Elder's Testimony—*Hatchet Lake*
27   How to Precipitate Yellowcake
28   Hatchet Lake Band's Testimony *(Erasure, Part Two)*
32   Cosmochemistry *(Part One)*
33   Elder's Testimony—*Clearwater River*
34   Water
35   Women's Testimony—*La Ronge*
36   Trapper's Testimony—*La Ronge*
39   Uraneco's Response—*La Ronge (Part One)*
40   Biologist's Response—*La Ronge (Part One)*
41   Uraneco's Response—*La Ronge (Part Two)*
42   Biologist's Response—*La Ronge (Part Two)*

| | |
|---|---|
| 43 | Uraneco's Response—*La Ronge (Part Three)* |
| 44 | Biologist's Response—*La Ronge (Part Three)* |
| 45 | Always Establish a Baseline |
| 46 | No Return |
| 47 | Métis Local 126's Testimony—*Saskatoon (Erasure)* |
| 50 | How to Sift the Many Metals? |
| 51 | Our Anger Is Radiant |
| 52 | Women's Testimony—*Saskatoon (Part One)* |
| 53 | Uraneco's Response—*Saskatoon* |
| 54 | Descent |
| 55 | Limnology |
| 56 | Collapse |
| 57 | Geophysicist's Testimony—*Saskatoon (Erasure)* |
| 58 | Rabbit Lake Fault |
| 59 | Call In the Dowsers, Now |
| 60 | Anthropocene |
| 61 | Cosmochemistry *(Part Two)* |
| 62 | Pyrocene |
| 63 | Biologist's Testimony re: White Oak Lake, Tennessee—*Regina (Erasure)* |
| 64 | We Dream Our Hands |
| 65 | Saskatoon Indigenous Coalition's Testimony—*Saskatoon* |
| 66 | Fallout |
| 67 | Will We Apologize? |
| 68 | Take It to the Light |
| 69 | Ethicist's Testimony—*Saskatoon* |
| 70 | Now, One Generation Later |
| 71 | Women's Testimony—*Saskatoon (Part Two)* |
| 73 | To Survive |
| 74 | Women's Testimony—*Saskatoon (Part Three)* |
| 75 | Our Fatigue Is the Future |
| | |
| 79 | *Notes* |
| 81 | *Acknowledgements* |

FOLLOW THE WATER

*Délı̨nę, Northwest Territories*

From the mouth of the widest river, along the shield's edge.
From the Great Lakes, northwest—

past Hudson Bay to the Beaufort Sea:
Winnipeg, Reindeer, Athabasca, Great Slave, Great Bear.

Fresh water runs on an angle, cuts across the continent.
Port Radium, northwest. Port Hope, southeast.

Mine and refinery.
Between: snake rivers, rail-line ladders

track the pageant from glacial retreat
to the hammered routes of trade.

## THE ROCK REVEALS ITSELF

*Délįnę, Northwest Territories*

To the seer, in his dream,
metal birds. A hole in the earth.

White-skinned men
descend and return.

A black rock.
An island.

An explosion
of light.

## LABINE

*Echo Bay, Great Bear Lake*

Saint Paul snow blind,
no charcoal on his cheeks.

A poultice of tea leaves over his eyes,
LaBine left him in the dark shack,
went to stake the claim.

A great wall seamed with silver, cobalt
bloom, copper green.

Marigold oxide on the black rock
like powdered sunshine lichen.

A piece of ore the size of a plum.
He knew it by its specific gravity:
solid pitchblende. Straining to hold

more energy than it could contain.
Throwing off gamma rays, errant vibrations
that penetrate in waves.

PITCHBLENDE

I.
At its surface, a cluster of electric clicks. A swarm of cicadas.
An underworld of endless X-rays. Read the radiograph,
    its staccato syntax scrambled
in accelerated rhythms.

II.
Waste rock. Slag. Greasy lustre stripped of silver veins, salvaged
for denser metals that conduct the cosmos from the earth's core
into the widening gyre.

III.
It withdraws, hastens. Makes the inhospitable home:
deserts, basins, barren lands.

IV.
A village of widows.
Broken ore in burlap.
A steamboat midway across Great Bear Lake.

V.
A map of the Manhattan Project:

| Echo Bay | Déline | Chalk River |
| | Hanford | Oak Ridge |
| | Los Alamos | Alamogordo |
| Hiroshima | Nagasaki | |

VI.
A secret kept by the basin, its people. A long story told in slow songs
of filtered silt as the lake bed sifts itself, listening.

VII.
Second-hand dust in wind blankets lichen,
collects in caribou liver and kidney.
Open pits deep enough to hold whole herds.

VIII.
The Dene ore carriers sleep on sacks of crushed rock.
Exhausted. The light inside them swallowed by stone, the sound
in a raven's glottal stop.

ENTER THE TRANSCRIPTS

A subterranean stream, a long reel of altered words, heard and reinterpreted, distant static running along a tapped ley line. Young women in federal offices, their names signed at the back of each text, attest they transcribed these words to the best of their abilities, each parenthetical inaudible not a failure, an admission, the best they could do, so many Elders in translation, many layers of mishearing already altering each speech, tipping the process toward a precipice, toward misprision. Read at your own risk. Words break down over time, travel from mind to mouth to ear to eye. What happens between: erosion, decay, necrosis.

## ELDER'S TESTIMONY

*Stony Rapids*

We are old. We have seen a lot.
We know when things are good
and when things are not.

We are people of the land. We need the land
to survive. We live like our ancestors.

Take our word and listen—
we will be thankful for that.

In the old days, if we set a short net
along the shore overnight,
we'd catch too many fish.

Now fish are disappearing
and wild animals are migrating away.

We worry there will be nothing left for us
once the mine has come and gone.

## INUIT TAPIRISAT OF CANADA'S TESTIMONY

*(Erasure)*

                                                                                                            beyond

    borders

(inaudible)

        caribou herds

                                                           crucial
                                            land claims

                            test

investigate
       (inaudible) process       (inaudible)
                                                              calving
grounds
                         (inaudible)
                                                  hearings

  whole

herds

                                    fallout

                        cadmium
                                                caribou


                        traditional land
threats                                     trust

LICHENOLOGY

Out of rock, they emerge.
Out of minerals, wood,

decomposition
deep in soil.

Fungus forms
mycological rhizomes,

foliose, fruticose, squamulose
lobes and crustose structures.

Fungus gives body
to algal bloom.

Lichens radiate from a central source,
spread at such a slow pace,

one could watch an entire lifetime
and never notice their movement.

## CARIBOU CONSERVATION BOARD'S TESTIMONY

*(Erasure)*


    herds                          tundra
        below

            beyond (inaudible)

        airborne                              habitats

             uranium
                  heavy metals

liver                                kidney
          radioactive    waters    leaked

                        across boundaries


                        (inaudible)

## THE NORTH IS NOT A BARREN LAND

Some see this province as straight lines, landlocked lakes of flax,
    highways
running past steamrolled horizon, grid road, rail track.

But just as the echoes of the Cypress Hills near Swift Current
spool off the tongue of a billion-year-old vibration,

the northern landscape troubles this mirage, undulates,
not a heat wave, a watermark, rippling surface.

Intricacy of riverwork, latticed waterways,
a system of lakes unlocked, knotted here and there,

pulse suppressed, energy tapped for cash, light.
Switches, ignitions. What comes from where?

So fixed on the dirtiest pits, we speak little about real needs. What we
    take without asking.
Assumptions we make about survival, sustenance, nourishment, luxury.

Food grows in the boreal forest: woodland caribou, moose,
spruce grouse, trout. Blueberry, cloudberry, bearberry, mossberry.
    Juniper. Currant. Indigo

milk caps, morels, chanterelles. Wild rice. Lichens.
People have fed and healed here for thousands of years.

Real needs are perceived by the heart and gut: edible berry,
    potable water.
Returning herd or spawning run. Body's response to rhythms around us.

Not the mind's design, not the thought that nags, *How much?*
How much? Enough.

# RABBIT LAKE URANIUM MINE

Eight hundred kilometres north of Saskatoon. Through mixed grassland, aspen parkland, boreal plain, boreal shield—the land metamorphoses from prairie to forest. Was the lake really named for a rabbit? Or was the word misheard? Hare Lake? Snowshoe? Jackrabbit? Not cottontail. White in winter. Longer in the leg and ear. Drained, mined, made a tailings pond. What's left of the lake whispers through sutures. Beneath, fear leaks, fills a forgotten stope. The hares left when the drilling began, running like white water, bleached and foamed. Smell of fear, acidic. A kick in the throat. Lungs and kidneys lined with a fine metallic film. Glimmer of trout scale: steelhead, rainbow.

## WHEN WOMEN SPEAK

*Hidden Bay*

They speak into a void, a pit,
its sides not precipitous but ridged.
A corkscrewed point of entry. A spiralling tunnel
through the lithosphere. Look into it:

milky green water, as if golden moonglow lichen
crushed and glittered into it. Their voices fragment,
merge, split again, reconfigure like beads
of mercury in the bottom of a tailings pond.

ORE BODY

We began to dig ourselves

deeper than we dreamed
when we began to see

metal as other than medicine,
our bodies, more than mineral.

Copper traces our skin,
iron, our blood.

Alkaline earth, our bones, teeth,
heartbeat. Potassium,

sodium, our pulse.
Sulphur. Selenium.

Zinc.

## ELDER'S TESTIMONY

*Black Lake*

Thank you for travelling
so far north.

We've been (inaudible) and we'd like to speak
our own language.

When we were young, there was no welfare. We made a living
trapping and fishing.

We understand water runs
under and around the mine.

We're worried uranium will ruin our water
as it has in the United States.

Old mines over at Uranium City
still pollute Athabascan lakes.

Our people never knew cancer
until the uranium mines came.

## URANECO'S RESPONSE

*Black Lake*

The Saskatchewan Cancer Registry does not have statistics
specific to Northern Saskatchewan or its Indigenous population.

The cancer that we see in these communities is most likely due
to an accumulation of insults on the body.

Conceivably, one could devise a system that would not discharge
contaminants into the environment,

but it might be too costly to operate.
So you have to consider that aspect.

Finally, I'd like to remind you, we're removing
the source of radioactivity from the area.

We're not putting it in; we're taking it out.
If anything, the region will be cleaner after we leave

because we'll be made to remove contaminants
that were there before mining began.

## DUST OR POLLEN

Uranium mines have ruined expanses of Dene land.
Speakers of Athabascan languages across this continent,
nomadic for millennia, Yukon to New Mexico.
Uranium mined, Port Radium to Church Rock.

A trail of choices: dust or pollen?

## FOND DU LAC

Bottom of the lake. End of the lake. Where Lake Athabasca, that major organ of water, narrows. Lake Athabasca, downstream from the tar sands. Uranium City, a scar on its northern shore. Such an expanse of land and water. Porous sandstone, deep aquifers, ground-fed lakes, subterranean streams. Land riven by water, lakes interrupted by islands. Each body, a point of entry, depression, low land, sunken, inundated, drowned. What lies beneath? Stories we never took seriously. Serpents. Yolks of their black eggs broken, golden, leak into the lake. Storm clouds gather within the earth. Detritus of weapons we should never have tested.

## ELDER'S TESTIMONY

*Fond du Lac*

These people that come up here
from Uraneco (inaudible).

We are northern people, (inaudible),
there are few of us, we are outnumbered.

We are just a handful of northern people up here.
New mines are (inaudible) around here.

We don't benefit from the mines.
People in the south benefit from the mines.

The money that comes from the work in the mines—
it can't buy caribou herds or clean lakes.
It can't remove radium from lichen.

## URANECO'S RESPONSE

*Fond du Lac*

Since 1975, we've mined 80 million
pounds of ore at Rabbit Lake.

Deposits under review hold
80 million more.

We'll hire up to 335 people
for at least 11 years.

That's 200 million in salaries,
77 million to northerners,

46 million to the Athabasca Basin
and 1.3 million to Fond du Lac.

## PARSE THE NUMBERS

A language of weight:
tonnes of ore, tens of thousands.

Wealth's overburden, its wages.
How to satisfy a world that wants to sleep

with lights on, heat high?
In the city, glass towers

glow from within all night.
Whole schools of light:

fluorescent, incandescent.
Halogen, ultraviolet. Black,

cathode blue. Limitless expansion.
Isn't this the myth we still whisper in our sleep?

We made light from stone
but only after we made it explode.

## HATCHET LAKE BAND'S TESTIMONY

*(Erasure, Part One)*

Elders

understand

        our ancestors

    land

                way of life

        understand

    the impact

        fish

              heavy

metals         in Hidden Bay
    radionuclides

        Hatchet Lake

                                            this risk

                                    lands

                       cyclical

                               damage

             if
      fish        if

                                        in
perpetuity

                                    local people


                                                        consequences

                        effluents    emissions
                water   air



                    local    fish

understand
                                                Athabasca

## ELDER'S TESTIMONY

*Hatchet Lake*

Caribou still come south
but the government tells us we can't eat the kidneys,

heavy with metals: cadmium, polonium, cesium, lead.
The government says it's okay to eat the liver.

Half a pound of meat per day, like getting a chest X-ray.
The government tells us this is natural—

radiation comes from sun, earth, air we breathe.
It all changes us. We just might not know until later.

## HOW TO PRECIPITATE YELLOWCAKE

Crush and bleach the black rock. Suck its shadow
until what's left is yellow dust, foreign pollen,
spores of disorder, death.

How to engineer an answer:
select what to measure, where.

Hire the experts.
Guide them in their work.

# HATCHET LAKE BAND'S TESTIMONY

*(Erasure, Part Two)*


              local people

                                      speak
                             free      words

                                  our people

  sparked

                       spill

       uranium

                  Elders

                     broken

  touched


        the mines
at Rabbit

```
            speak
            heart


                        speak

                                    dispute
                                challenge
                                                    after the
   mines          land and water
              we have to live              our lives
   our children              their lives
                        future


                        the spill                       travels


                    tailings                        a river

       a spill                                              spill
                                            to speak

                    the spill




                                    two million litres of radioactive
       water
```

                                              broader
                                              broader
                                        other countries
　　　Dene                                              Navajo
　　　communities




                                        royalty shares
　　　　Treaty Rights



                                              shut down

                                        shut down
　　　　democratic
                                  nuclear waste
                                        bury it


                                                    health
　　future      children              health

                                                    health
              future
　　　health
                                                    destroying
                        creating
                  making

an open mind

                              believe
                              think
                              speak
                speak         speak

                      love

## COSMOCHEMISTRY

*(Part One)*

Before language,
our galaxy opened

a black hole at its core.

Born in sudden light,
the sound of our eruption

dampened by expansion.

We began in an explosion,
borne by death.

Empty space scintillating.

We began in clouds
of dust and gas.

## ELDER'S TESTIMONY

*Clearwater River*

Animals keep us alive, allow us to survive.
When animals begin to disappear,
we know humans will soon disappear, too.

This is what we must consider:
earth is alive, land is our mother,
mining kills fresh water.

We don't have a voice:
Indian Affairs runs the reservations,
chief and council make decisions.
Those who want mines get them.

WATER

What sets our planet apart. Allows our survival. Where our story begins and ends. Creation myths, floods, yet the world will end in fire. Fire that finds its way into water. Fire that takes water's form and spreads, beneath the earth's surface, subterranean, unseen. Invisible fire that cannot be smothered or doused. Those it singes don't know they've swallowed the sun until mouths fill with cinders, marrow turns to ash. Not only the taps near the fracking fields leaking flammable gas, but the northern waters, those in which fish still spawn, those we spin into gold, dammed. Waters we consume at a rate the rest of the world can hardly imagine. Waters we contaminate, break.

## WOMEN'S TESTIMONY

*La Ronge*

There have been spills. We don't know
how many. Half a million litres, at least.

They say it was run-off
from spring melt. They say

there was radium in the muskeg
before they arrived.

We have no confidence in Uraneco.
The more we learn, the less we trust.

## TRAPPER'S TESTIMONY

*La Ronge*

So the Uranium Mining Medicine Show is back
to trade us money for radioactive rocks.

We've had so many of these hearings, I can't keep track.
So many mines going in, soon the Athabasca Basin will be one big pit,

and every time it's the same line: we've got to approve this or else
fire every worker and put the industry out of business.

It's all bullshit. They'll make up whatever
numbers they need to convince us we need these mines.

I've worked up north all my life and never in a mine.
It's the mines that might take my livelihood away.

I fish and trap and keep asking the same damn questions:
what were the lakes like before the first mine and what are they like now?

Show me a baseline study,
show me the cumulative effects.

Do these people even know which way the water flows?
Do they know Wollaston Lake drains in two directions?

The corporations and governments care about money.
I care about water. We don't need uranium; we need water.

In the future, wars will be fought over fresh water,
and we've got more than 100,000 lakes up here.

But we're pumping radioactive effluent into them.
We're pumping ammonia and arsenic into them.

Our water is more valuable than all the mines combined.
Water is the fishery, the food chain. Our bodies

are made of water. We can't live without it.
We can't drink water laced with arsenic and radium.

I'd like to see Uraneco go downstream from the site
with a tin cup and have a taste.

I haven't written much down here. I'm speaking from what I know.
That Environmental Impact Statement made no sense to me,

so I can't speak to any of the specific issues in it.
Maybe if it weren't just a long list of numbers,

maybe if it were written in plain English
and said whether the tailing ponds still leak,
whether the water is still so acidic, it's dead.

What good are those numbers to the Dene and Cree
when they still live on that land?

What good are those numbers
when no baseline study was ever done?

Until Uraneco answers two simple questions,
our only option is civil disobedience.

Tell us what the water was like before you started to mine
and tell us what the effects will be over time.

If you can't answer these questions, we'll blockade the roads.
We've done it before. We'll do it again.

I don't have the cash to take these people to court.
No fisherman or trapper in Northern Saskatchewan
has money for lawyers and legal fees.

Let's not kid ourselves: the governments and corporations
make the decisions. We can talk the ears off these panel members

and they can recommend some precautionary measures
but we can't count on the corporations.

Our governments are supposed to protect us
but instead they give the corporations whatever they want.

I'm not here for personal reasons. This isn't self-interest.
It won't bother me if all that waste escapes

because I won't be here long enough to suffer from it.
It's the water I worry about. The water that has been here for
    millions of years.

Fresh water. Ground water. Lakes and streams.
Once that water dies, it's only a matter of time
before everything else dies too.

URANECO'S RESPONSE

*La Ronge (Part One)*

It's difficult, a document like this.

An assessment.
A statement of impact.

Burdened by technical details, too many

for the ordinary reader,
too few for the regulators.

The reason for these hearings:

a middle road not walked,
or not walked well.

BIOLOGIST'S RESPONSE

*La Ronge (Part One)*

So many question marks,
                 gaps in Uraneco's data.

They can't tell us how the site has changed,
                 what impact their operation has had,
because the site was not properly studied
                 before mining began.
No baseline was ever established.

URANECO'S RESPONSE

*La Ronge (Part Two)*

We have environmental data from Rabbit Lake
collected over eighteen years in seven different reports,

such as the Hidden Bay Report of 1973
or the Beaver and Muskrat Survey of 1976.

We did study the site, and obviously our data were accepted
because the regulators permitted us to proceed.

Now standards have changed, and we're being asked questions
that no one thought to ask when we first began our work.

So it's unfortunate that we're not able to answer
but there's no going back now; we can only move forward.

## BIOLOGIST'S RESPONSE

*La Ronge (Part Two)*

It's true standards have been raised,
                    which is why you must do more
to set scientists at ease,
                    enable us to trust you.

We need to understand the system
                    holistically, the many relationships
between sediments and insects,
                    insects and fish.

There's a direct connection
                    between the fish we eat and the lake's benthic layers.
If heavy metals and radioactive materials
                    accumulate in those layers, they move through
                          the food chain
into our mouths.

## URANECO'S RESPONSE

*La Ronge (Part Three)*

The Athabasca Basin communities

did not express concerns
about insects and sediments.

They expressed concerns about water and fish

and our samples indicate
we have not harmed either of these.

BIOLOGIST'S RESPONSE

    *La Ronge (Part Three)*


I believe the people of the north are worried
                about more than just water and fish.
I believe they're worried
                about the entire ecosystem.
Not only their land and traplines,
                but all connections between.

## ALWAYS ESTABLISH A BASELINE

A bass line, a thrumming rhythm.
A point of departure,

and then the echo opens
like a dying star.

Even-keeled. Drop-kicked,
cyclical.

Now wait, and watch
for fallout.

## NO RETURN

There is no going back. Only forward. Return the land to its First Peoples. We have forgotten the spiral, the long circuit, the return to a place similar but altered, each season, cycle of each day. Land will heal, cultures evolve, emerge from the land, its wounds. Cultures grown from those older than our own—these will heal the land. There is no erasing this history. There will be no more forgetting: land scarred, visible from satellites, bleached tracts of dust, low structures, pits. Open pits. Craters. As if the Athabasca Basin were struck by a series of meteors. As if the ore bodies were foreign, in need of excision. Astroblemes. As if we'd known all along this ore is cosmologically other. Ancient dust from dying stars. Excision sites, scars.

## MÉTIS LOCAL 126'S TESTIMONY

*Saskatoon (Erasure)*


White


        capitalists        extract




                          children

                Stanley Mission, Weyakwin, Timber Bay, Uranium City




vortex
poverty

        capitalist economy                                 beginning
in the 1700s                                        the Hudson's Bay
Company             profits before people
                                  technocratic

                                           neo-corporate colonization


                                         profit     at the
expense of    people                       at the expense of the land



                Gulf Minerals


                            millions of dollars
                                                        make
more jails

          end    exploitation
      restore          communities displaced

     compensation
    for damage


  coercive in nature




forests                lakes

                        nuclear
  waste                  tough    luck

## HOW TO SIFT THE MANY METALS?

Lead in the lake bed's silt
sinks so swiftly.

No sieve made for this,
except a fish's liver

or its mouthful of mud.
A skiff skims the surface

in slow circles, mirrors
the microscope's myopic lens.

What won't the single sample show?
The many pathways radium takes

as it decays. Always, there is more,
unseen, travelling below at the pace of stone.

Changes accumulate, accrue in increments,
inching outward into the unknown.

## OUR ANGER IS RADIANT

Not just the finish on our skin beneath this fluorescent ceiling or the luminous glass of our eyes as our throats constrict while we speak, no, it is a heavy tone materializing in the air between us. It is filling the room. Soon the room will be trembling with it. It will tighten us all until we become fixed where we stand, sit. Our anger is elemental. It is coming through us from beneath our feet. We cannot contain it. We do not control it. It will spread, a kind of liquid fire. Something between gasoline and flame. See it glow and wait for it to explode.

# WOMEN'S TESTIMONY

### *Saskatoon (Part One)*

Tailings leak. Tailings leak
        and water spreads
in intricate networks
        beyond our borders.

We cannot contain it. We do not control it.
The industry wants to focus on money.
But money flows beyond our borders, too.

Unsustainable, non-renewable
        capitalist industries
destabilize communities,
        displace traditional economies.

We don't need to believe Uraneco
when they tell us this is our only choice.

We could be so much more
        self-sufficient. We need to change
the way we think. Expect less,
        accept what we have.

## URANECO'S RESPONSE

*Saskatoon*

We took the Elders under Rabbit Lake
to show them it was safe.

Nineteen Dene Elders
from the three northern basin bands:
Hatchet Lake, Black Lake, Fond du Lac.

They didn't understand
how we could mine below a lake

but there we were, metres of rock
between us and the water.

No limits to what we can do
now. No ore body in this basin

we can't excavate. A lake
isn't an obstacle. We know

what we're doing.
We'll show you.

DESCENT

A mechanical act, a question of physics.
Not the underworld but its antechamber.
Archean basement.

What comes before the fire:
air thick with dust. Lake silt. Soot.
The fire, a slow explosion.

Waterborne. Airborne.
Cells mushroom, bloom.

LIMNOLOGY

Up north, the land is porous, sandstone.

Deep aquifers, ground-fed lakes,
subterranean rivers and streams

travel great distances, change
continuously. Sinuous and mercurial.

Water has a mind of its own.

Mining fractures and refracts
fault lines, weakens rifts.

What echoes outward, upward.
Sound of hooves, thunder.

COLLAPSE

Occurs close to the earth,
from cracks in its foundation.

Lowest orders fall first.
Roots die at their deepest.

Oldest and earliest.
Invertebrates.

Smallest and softest,
some barely visible.

Shells coiled in codes.
Exoskeletons exposed.

## GEOPHYSICIST'S TESTIMONY

*Saskatoon (Erasure)*

                                                        worldwide
                              ignore
      geologists

        past
                masks

                                                                             inhale


                                ore bodies
        toxic elements

                                          quicksilver
cobalt
              can kill
                  miners

                              pale
dead men

        worldwide                        menacing
        anomalies
          agencies                      arsenic

## RABBIT LAKE FAULT

The industry says it is stable, ancient. They say the same
about the Ghost Dance Fault, where it runs under Yucca Mountain's
   waste.

Salt mines in the south already cause small earthquakes in previously
   stable plates.
What echoes outward, upward? Sound of hooves, thunder, lightning
   strikes.

Billions of years older than coal, more abundant than gold, this ore
emits a low electromagnetic drone.

The ecology of rock. Something we hardly considered. The vibrations
we radiate, tonal, discordant. Our bodies, ore bodies, orogenies,

buried in earth, emerge, return. Tip the balance, volatile. Trigger
new patterns of collapse, cycles of decay.

People are afraid of the future north littered with ghost towns,
   dead streams,
poorly decommissioned pits, stockpiles of waste rock, tailings.

What happens after the exodus? After the last tonne of ore is taken
from the basin? Will we bury the cylinders here? Fissionless missiles,

spent yet still too hot to touch. Will we hang hollow bones to warn
   the unborn?
Mark the sites with moose skulls? Caribou vertebrae?

Will their sound in the wind be worn down, drowned out
by the endless electromagnetic drone?

## CALL IN THE DOWSERS, NOW

Ghosts in these waters, thin
streams, pale filaments—not algal bloom
but spirits pulled, thread-like, not annelids,
but their echoes:

the sounds of ancient earthquakes,
unstable tectonic plates,
waves of movement,
successions.

Patterns repeat.
Ghost Dance Fault.
Rabbit Lake Fault.
Earth opens.

## ANTHROPOCENE

We can't just consume; we need to conserve.
Heat, seeds. Generate more of our own light.
Burn beeswax, breathe fireweed.
Forage, ferment. Remember darkness

teaches us to listen. Sleep less in summer,
more in winter. This is our future. Night
accelerates and the outer limits of the cosmos
drift farther from shore. A lengthening exhale.

We are consumptive. Blood in our lungs. Tar.
Radiotoxic dust. Coal, shale, oil, ore.
We crack the ancient world's ribs
for our one last gasp.

COSMOCHEMISTRY

    *(Part Two)*


What lies beyond the earth and sky?

Realms from which this radiant rock arrived.
Pillars of dust. Distant light. Innumerable nebulae.

How long will we live?
The rock will remain.

How long have we lived?
In the story of life on earth?
An instant.

What came before?
Multitudes. Long reels of annelids,
the ammonite and coelacanth.

What will outlive us?
Some of the above. None of the above.
Eventually, all will return to dust.
Our sun is set to swallow us.

PYROCENE

Our own star was never enough for us. We were envious
of the sky's thin white fire. Flint's fricative shift, the sound of it
catching, spirant. Sudden rush of breath.

First we burned wood, then whole forests
that died before we took form. Coal-fired.
Carboniferous. Ancient heat beneath our feet.

BIOLOGIST'S TESTIMONY
RE: WHITE OAK LAKE, TENNESSEE

    *Regina (Erasure)*


    Oak Ridge                              radioactive
                      since 1943

              the lake    lithic
cesium             insects, fish      snails

                             aquatic plants
     accumulate radioactivity and release it


fish—uranium and strontium     taken in by bone


    malignancies


           (inaudible),
      elements enter sediments
                   Clinch River       Chalk
River
                    cobalt
        cesium
      cesium
                 cesium

## WE DREAM OUR HANDS

corrode from the inside out.
Palms open like pits. Marrow turned
acidic, burning through bone.

The data never did determine
exactly how fast this happens.
How much time it takes to decay.

No measurement—
microrems or millisieverts,
picocuries or becquerels—
no accurate unit for fear.

## SASKATOON INDIGENOUS COALITION'S TESTIMONY

    *Saskatoon*

Mining, refining, weapons and waste—
worldwide, Indigenous people are first and hardest hit.

North America:
Cree, Dene, Métis, Ojibwe,
Lakota, Navajo, Shoshone, Paiute, among others,
have suffered and survived mining, waste and testing.
Australia: mining and testing.

South Pacific: more testing.

Costs outweigh benefits: cleaning up and storing toxic waste.
Long-term health care for cancer.

Government records do not reflect the damage done
    by the nuclear industry.
Little epidemiological evidence exists.

The people of Saskatchewan's north have never been given a choice.
This is coercive development. This is not consensual.
Mines were active before these hearings began.

## FALLOUT

Smoke from northern fires drifts south.
Winds, indiscriminate, prevail.

Fallout from Chernobyl. Fallout
from Soviet tests.

Boreal forest, a shroud
around the shoulders of the world.
A lamp left burning.

Sand from southern winds drifts north. Fallout
from Nevada's test site once dusted Saskatchewan's south.
Nearly a thousand explosions over forty years.

Grain in wind shimmered an electric desert sheen.
You couldn't see it or smell it, but the radon hung in your lungs

like mist in a coulee, waiting to precipitate
like salt in an alkaline slough.

Every tilled tract of land. How soil breathes.
Gases that catch and release.

## WILL WE APOLOGIZE?

Decades from now when we learn where it went,
how many cells mushroomed like yucca blooms

in the basin. Will we assume a radical sense of responsibility?
The way the Dene Elders did in their apology to the Hibakusha

because rock from their lake shore helped build those bombs.
Will we resist complacency? Squint into this searing flash?

Will we admit we are all complicit?

## TAKE IT TO THE LIGHT

Where power was made, lamps lit, bury it there. Bury it where light was made, power consumed, where fumes, rays, faded. Let those who use it bear its waste, those who live with the wounds heal the land. We need generations of keepers and guardians for decommissioned mine sites, deep geological repositories. Glassified thorium. Mausoleums of light. We've rearranged whole ore bodies, used them as fuel, used them in fields of fluorescence, in cancer treatments. Irradiated seeds, detonated weapons: atmospheric, oceanic, underground. Tests, tests, tests. How we fail. How we pass.

ETHICIST'S TESTIMONY

*Saskatoon*

Uraneco sells uranium
to countries that have refused to sign
the Non-Proliferation Treaty,

including France, which continues to test
nuclear weapons in the South Pacific.

Uraneco claims our uranium is used for peaceful purposes:
electricity, diagnostic tests, medical isotopes, X-rays—
but most of it leaves the country.

Perhaps the panel isn't interested in the impact
our mines have on other countries,
but the fact is, Saskatchewan's uranium ends up far beyond our borders.

The United States' Atoms for Peace Treaty promises
not to use Canadian uranium in weapons,

but we know that depleted Canadian uranium has gone
into armour-piercing bullets used in combat in Iraq.
Still radioactive, these shells now scatter the desert.

Uraneco says Canada's safeguards are some of the strictest in the world,
but the truth is, they aren't strict at all.

NOW, ONE GENERATION LATER

Cancer rates in heavily shelled cities like Basra and Fallujah have increased exponentially. Not only since the early nineties. But again since 2004. Predominantly childhood cancers, namely leukemia. Writing from the future. Writing looking back in time, not simply over the shoulder, but turning toward it and feeling consumed by the heat searing off of it. Another explosion out in the desert. What our planet must look like from a great distance, a reel of film, sped up and looped. The flashes like pinpoint erasures. Something disappearing and then reappearing filtered through grungy screens of smoke and ash. As if the stub end of a pencil pressed and spun. We come out in the wash of time frail and harder to recognize. We are becoming fragments. Bones corroding just like we fevered. The sound of hooves again, echolocating their origin across the night sky.

## WOMEN'S TESTIMONY

### *Saskatoon (Part Two)*

This hearing process is based on a win-lose conflict model.
This is not mediation. This is not principled negotiation.

In this process, we have been polarized,
made to face each other as rivals.

We don't need to argue and compete. We need to talk.
We need to cooperate, help each other
reach consensus.

A principled approach would focus on our needs
and desires; it would focus on our fears.

This isn't possible here
because this panel's mandate is so strictly limited.

We can't talk about where uranium goes, how it's used;
we can't talk about alternatives.

We can't even talk about how extraction
really affects our aquifer, watershed—
no one has the data.

After so many hearings, we are exhausted.

Each new mine means a new hearing, a new panel.
There are many corporations at work up north,
which means new faces at the table every time.

But we don't get a break.
There could have been one big hearing
to determine whether we wanted this or not
but we didn't get it.

Many of us don't trust this process.
That's why there are fewer people here.

Our energy is lagging.
We are worn out.

TO SURVIVE

To continue to live or exist, especially in spite of danger or hardship. Our planet has a lifespan. It is halfway through its spiral and the gyre continues to widen. We will either explode or be swallowed. The energy that we are will disperse and resurface. Here, now, we have the life of the mine, the lives of its miners, its wastes, but we can hardly see 10,000 years behind us, the paths we walked through glacial retreat. Life began so slowly. In our earliest forms, we were almost imperceptible. Small groups of us moved across lands that opened as the skies closed. Time looped through itself, tidal. Days lengthened and shortened and lengthened again. Dark matter—how to measure its movement from moment to moment? How to chart its shift through the many millennia?

## WOMEN'S TESTIMONY

### *Saskatoon (Part Three)*

This whole process is flawed—
our governments and their regulatory agencies support
    the nuclear industry.

Our governments protect corporations, they protect profits.
They do not protect people.

That's why this public record is crucial:
the transcripts will reveal that despite limitations,

these hearings allowed us to express ourselves
and for that we are grateful.

## OUR FATIGUE IS THE FUTURE

A weighted quilt stuffed with irradiated goose down. We are sleeping under it, dreaming of water. The glitter of it early in the morning or late in the day. They thought the sun was rising on a new era, visions of this liquid white heat churning like the underside of a steamship. This would be better than any railroad ever was, better than any wind farm or solar field. Their future was something they imagined illustrated in a magazine glorifying the Anthropocene. An article never to be written because we know now what we knew then. Nothing has changed. It has only grown heavier and harder. Harder to look away and pretend we hadn't seen it coming clear as the sunrise. It's setting now. The sun upon the story. A layer of something neatly woven. Thin strips of bark from larch and aspen. Our fatigue is the way fingers feel, rubbing the thinness from what's left of a day. We say we are tired and what we mean is there is very little light left for us to make here. You'll need to find your own flint from here on in.

NOTES

I wrote the poems in *Pitchblende* after reading testimonies given at public hearings held throughout Saskatchewan in 1993 on the territories of Treaties 4, 6, 8, and 10. These testimonies can be found in published transcripts archived at the University of Saskatchewan in several volumes totalling nearly two thousand pages.

I have adapted sections of testimony, while also writing poems triggered by their content and related research. As I distilled the transcripts, I came to envision this project as a political intervention and I chose to focus on the extent to which the needs, desires, and fears of those who chose to testify publicly and on record continue to be dismissed and diminished by the neocolonial machine, which promotes profit and industry at the expense of community and sustainability.

The Rabbit Lake hearings were structured in a way that favoured privileged speakers: members of the corporate proponents' panel were white male settlers; members of the federally appointed panel were also exclusively male and only one member was of Indigenous ancestry. By favouring the voices of Indigenous Elders and a united group of women (who were white settlers), I sought to disrupt this discourse and provide an alternative lens: a way of seeing through and beyond the binary opposition of "economy" and "ecology."

Throughout the transcripts, passages of inaudibility are marked in parentheses. I attempt to use these instances of inaudibility as points of aperture into a parallel unspoken and unrecorded text. The inclusion of these "(inaudible)" passages found in the transcripts, as well as erasures, is intended to draw the reader's attention toward what was misheard or left unsaid at the hearings, as well as to the perceived silence of the mineral world.

ACKNOWLEDGEMENTS

Thank you to the Interdisciplinary Centre for Culture and Creativity and the College of Graduate Studies and Research at the University of Saskatchewan, as well as the Social Sciences and Humanities Research Council of Canada for their support. Thank you to my supervisor Dr. Hilary Clark, my thesis mentor Sheri Benning, my program coordinator Dr. Jeanette Lynes, and my peers in the Master of Fine Arts in Writing at the University of Saskatchewan for their support and suggestions, especially Mika Lafond for putting me in touch with Rita Bouvier and Simon Bird. I would also like to thank Dr. Priscilla Settee and Rita Bouvier for speaking with me and responding to my concerns about appropriation as per the use of Indigenous Elders' testimonies found in the transcripts.

Special thanks to Randy Lundy for his encouragement and insight in editing, as well as to Karen Clark and Kelly Laycock for all their editorial assistance. I would also like to thank the editors of the following literary journals and anthologies for publishing earlier versions of these poems: *filling Station, Grain Magazine, OK Magpie, Room Magazine, Ryga: A Journal of Provocations, Understorey,* and *30 Under 30: An Anthology of Canadian Millennial Poets.*

This work was influenced by ecocritical theory and ecofeminist theory, as well as by rhizome theory, as laid out in Gilles Deleuze and Félix Guattari's *A Thousand Plateaus*. I have also been influenced by Don McKay's concept of "geopoetics" outlined in *Deactivated West 100* and by Sue Goyette's experiments with appropriating and altering government documents in *Outskirts*. I would like to thank Sandy Pool for her work *Undark: An Oratorio* and my friend Chelsea Rushton for bringing it to my attention. I would also like to thank Mikaela Dyke for her play *Dying Hard*, based on the testimony of dying fluorspar miners. I have also indirectly quoted W.B. Yeats in using the phrase "widening gyre" in the title poem and again in "To Survive."

I would like to acknowledge that these poems were written on Treaty 6 territory in central Saskatchewan and edited on unceded Coast Salish territory. I am grateful for my time spent as an uninvited guest on Treaty 6 land and for everything I learned there during that time, as well as for the time I continue to spend and learning I continue to receive on unceded Coast Salish land.

Author proceeds from this book will be donated to the Eli Fleury Cultural Centre at Northlands College in La Ronge, Saskatchewan.

Elise Marcella Godfrey's poetry has appeared in literary journals such as *subTerrain*, *Room*, *Prism*, and *Grain*. Her relationship with uranium began with a piece of pitchblende she acquired in Nelson, BC, in 2008. This piece of pitchblende, originally from Great Bear Lake, was identified and surrendered to a secure site at the University of Saskatchewan while writing the poems in this book. A white settler, Elise now lives with her family on the ancestral, traditional, and unceded land of the Qayqayt First Nation.

ᐅᓄᑲ

## OSKANA POETRY & POETICS
### BOOK SERIES

Publishing new and established authors, Oskana Poetry & Poetics offers both contemporary poetry at its best and probing discussions of poetry's cultural role.

Randy Lundy—*Series Editor*

*Advisory Board*

| | | |
|---|---|---|
| Sherwin Bitsui | Louise Bernice Halfe | Duane Niatum |
| Robert Bringhurst | Tim Lilburn | Gary Snyder |
| Laurie D. Graham | | Karen Solie |

For more information about publishing in the series, please see:
www.uofrpress.ca/poetry

**PREVIOUS BOOKS IN THE SERIES:**

*Measures of Astonishment: Poets on Poetry,* presented by the League of Canadian Poets (2016)

*The Long Walk,* by Jan Zwicky (2016)

*Cloud Physics,* by Karen Enns (2017)

*The House of Charlemagne,* by Tim Lilburn (2018)

*Blackbird Song,* by Randy Lundy (2018)

*Forty-One Pages: On Poetry, Language and Wilderness,* by John Steffler (2019)

*Live Ones,* by Sadie McCarney (2019)

*Field Notes for the Self,* by Randy Lundy (2020)

*Burden,* by Douglas Burnet Smith (2020)

*Red Obsidian,* by Stephan Torre (2021)

www.ingramcontent.com/pod-product-compliance
Lightning Source LLC
Chambersburg PA
CBHW032046290426
44110CB00012B/977